Grover Cleveland

BY REBECCA RISSMAN

The Child's World®
childsworld.com

Published by The Child's World®
1980 Lookout Drive • Mankato, MN 56003-1705
800-599-READ • www.childsworld.com

ISBN 9781503816466
LCCN 2016945657

Printed in the United States of America
PAO2322

ABOUT THE AUTHOR

Rebecca Rissman is a nonfiction author and editor. She has written more than 200 books about history, science, and art. She lives in Chicago, Illinois, with her husband and two daughters. She enjoys hiking, yoga, and cooking.

Table of Contents

Grover Cleveland was the 22nd president of the United States.

CHAPTER ONE

The Veto President

★ ★ ★

It was 1885. Grover Cleveland was president of the United States. The country was healing from the Civil War. The war had been deadly. Many men had been wounded. Some were too hurt to work. They could not earn enough to live. So the government gave them money. These payments helped them buy what they needed.

Some men were not as hurt. But they still wanted money. They lied to the government.

They said they were wounded badly. Cleveland did not believe them. He read the **applications** for the payments himself. He wanted to give money only to those badly hurt. This was a big job. He read hundreds of applications a day.

Cleveland turned down many applications. This angered the soldiers. They wanted money. They felt the government owed them.

However, not everyone was angry. Some Americans were happy about it. They thought the government needed to save money. They did not like wasteful government spending.

Cleveland hated wasting money, too. He **vetoed** anything he thought was too expensive. He turned down many government ideas. He became known as "the Veto President."

Congress thought Cleveland was too tough. The soldiers were voters. Congressmen wanted them on their side. Congress passed a new bill for government payments. Cleveland shut down that bill, too. Cleveland stayed true to his **beliefs**.

The New Jersey house where Cleveland was born

CHAPTER TWO

The Early Years

Stephen Grover Cleveland was born on March 18, 1837. He was from Caldwell, New Jersey. Grover's family was poor. He was one of nine children. Grover's father died when he was 16. Grover quit school when this happened. He worked to provide for his family.

Cleveland was interested in law. He became a lawyer in 1859. He moved to Buffalo, New York.

Then Cleveland was needed in the U.S. Civil War. But his mother was sick. She needed help. Cleveland paid another man to fight in his place.

Cleveland was nominated for president at the 1884 Democratic Convention.

This was allowed at the time. He stayed home and helped his family.

Cleveland was a successful lawyer. He was well respected. He decided to run for office. He became mayor of Buffalo in 1881.

In 1883, he became governor of New York. He ran as a **Democrat**.

Cleveland valued honesty. He thought **politicians** should tell the truth.

The Democrats in New York were powerful. Cleveland took away many of their special **benefits**. He worked to fight dishonesty. Many New York Democrats turned against him.

Then Cleveland wanted to run for president. This was a hard decision. The New York Democrats wanted him to lose. Cleveland entered the race in 1884. He ran against James G. Blaine. Blaine was a Republican.

Many people did not like Blaine. Republicans who did not back him voted for Cleveland. Many Democrats from other states did, too. Cleveland won the **election**. He became president in 1885.

Cleveland was the first Democrat to be elected president in more than 30 years.

CHAPTER THREE

Cleveland's First Term

Cleveland wanted things in government to be fair. Sometimes Congress gave special favors to certain people. Cleveland tried to stop this. It took a lot of effort. He often worked until after midnight.

In 1886, Cleveland got married. His wife's name was Frances Folsom. Cleveland was the first president to get married in the White House. The wedding took place on the first floor. It was small and simple.

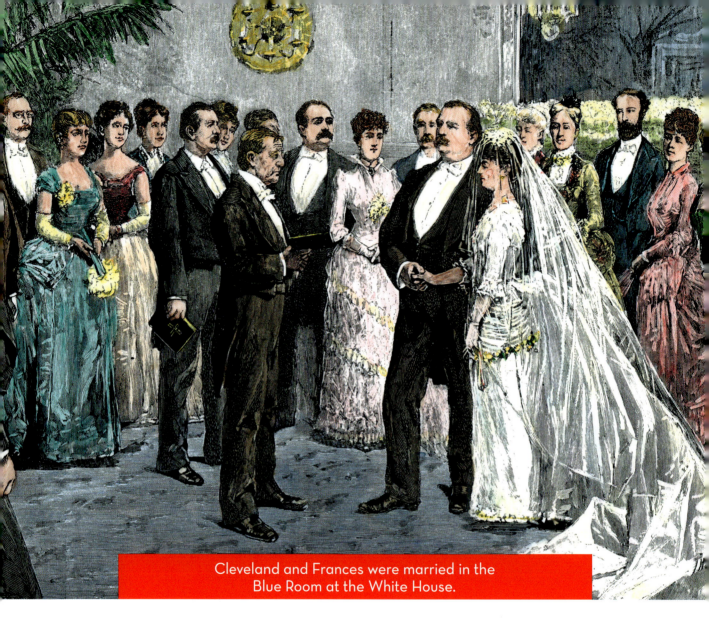

Cleveland and Frances were married in the Blue Room at the White House.

Only 28 guests were there. Frances soon became famous. People bought postcards with her picture on them.

Cleveland made many hard decisions as president. Sometimes his choices made people angry. Once, he discovered that railroad companies had stolen government land. He made them return it. This upset the railroad owners. But Cleveland did not care. He believed the president should not be afraid of upsetting people.

Cleveland continued to save the government money. In 1887, hot weather killed many crops in Texas. Farmers were struggling. Some were very poor. Congress tried to pass a bill. It would give the farmers money. But Cleveland turned it down. He did not think the government should help. He thought the farmers should take care of themselves.

Many voters did not like Cleveland's actions. He ran for a second **term** in 1888. He lost. A Republican named Benjamin Harrison won instead.

Cleveland is the only president to serve
two terms that were not in a row.

CHAPTER FOUR

Cleveland's Second Term

Cleveland moved back to New York. He worked at a law firm. Then he was asked to run for president again. He agreed. He won in 1892.

Cleveland moved back to the White House. The country was in trouble. Many people needed jobs. Businesses were struggling. Cleveland tried to fix things. He worked with banks and businesses. It did not help. Americans were angry with Cleveland.

More than 12,000 troops were sent to end the Pullman Strike of 1894.

They thought he valued businesses over people. But he did not give in.

Cleveland had another problem in 1894. Railroad workers in Chicago, Illinois, were angry. They wanted to be paid more. They also wanted to be treated better. So they went on **strike**. It was called the Pullman Strike. Trains stopped running. This made Cleveland mad. The government needed the trains. Trains carried things like the mail. Cleveland sent the Army to Chicago. They tried to make the workers return to their jobs. But things got worse. The workers started fighting the Army soldiers. Many people were hurt or killed.

Cleveland understood why the railroad workers were angry. He believed they should be treated better. But he also wanted them to keep working.

Other workers across the country were upset, too. They also felt overworked and underpaid.

Many asked the government to make a holiday. It would be a day workers would take off. But they would still get paid. Cleveland signed the bill in August 1894. The holiday honors the country's workers. It is called Labor Day.

By 1896, many Americans turned against Cleveland. They thought he did not help the country enough. He even lost the support of the Democratic party.

Cleveland returned to New Jersey. It was the end of his term. He went to work at Princeton University. Cleveland helped run the school. He also taught classes.

Cleveland died on June 24, 1908. He had been ill for a long time.

Cleveland and Frances with their four children, Esther, Francis, Marion, and Richard

Cleveland was honored in many ways. His face appeared on the $1,000 bill. He was a strong leader with bold ideas. He always stood firm for his beliefs.

1830

←── **March 18, 1837** Stephen Grover Cleveland is born in Caldwell, New Jersey.

←── **October 1, 1853** Cleveland's father dies.

←── **November 1881** Cleveland is elected mayor of Buffalo, New York.

←── **November 7, 1882** Cleveland is elected governor of New York.

←── **November 4, 1884** Cleveland beats James G. Blaine and is elected president.

←── **June 2, 1886** Cleveland marries Frances Folsom at the White House.

←── **November 6, 1888** Cleveland loses the presidential election to Benjamin Harrison.

←── **November 8, 1892** Cleveland beats Benjamin Harrison and is elected president for a second term.

←── **May 11, 1894** The Pullman Strike begins in Chicago, Illinois.

←── **June 24, 1908** Cleveland dies in New Jersey.

1910

applications (ap-luh-KAY-shuhns) Applications are written requests for something. Cleveland turned down many applications for government payments.

beliefs (bih-LEEFS) Beliefs are an opinion or faith in something. Cleveland stayed true to his beliefs.

benefits (BEN-uh-fits) Benefits are advantages or things that are helpful. Cleveland took away the special benefits given to members of New York Democrats.

Congress (KON-gress) Congress is the branch of the U.S. government that makes laws. Congress tried to pass many laws while Cleveland was president.

Democrat (DEM-uh-krat) A Democrat is a member of the Democratic political party. Cleveland was a Democrat.

politicians (pol-i-TISH-uhns) Politicians are people who seek or hold public office positions. Cleveland wanted to stop politicians from being dishonest.

strike (STRIKE) A strike occurs when employees stop working to prove a point or bring attention to an issue. Railroad workers in Chicago went on strike to protest their low pay.

term (TERM) A term is a period of time an official serves in office. Cleveland was elected to his first term as president in 1884.

vetoed (VEE-tohd) When something is vetoed, it is rejected or turned down. Cleveland vetoed so many bills that he became known as "the Veto President."

In the Library

Bausum, Ann. *Our Country's Presidents.*
New York City: National Geographic, 2013.

Burns, Ken. *Grover Cleveland, Again!* New York City: Knopf Books, 2016.

Cleveland, Will. *Yo, Millard Fillmore! (And All Those Other Presidents You Don't Know)* Westport, CT: Prospecta Press, 2014.

On the Web

Visit our Web site for links about
Grover Cleveland: **childsworld.com/links**

Note to Parents, Teachers, and Librarians: We routinely verify our Web links to make sure they are safe and active sites. So encourage your readers to check them out!

INDEX